# That Ship Has Sailed!

by Mrs. Clausen-Grace's class
with Tony Stead

capstone

# Introduction

*by Delilah and Eden*

You've heard of Neil Armstrong, but have you heard of Leif Eriksson? From the beginning of time, there have been explorers of all kinds. These explorers all had their similarities. They inspired, they conquered, they made discoveries, but most of all, they made differences that changed the world around them. Explorers have soared as high as Amelia Earhart, dove down deep like Sylvia Earle, and battled fiercely like Zhang Qian. What did they find? What did they do? Turn the page to find out!

MAR DEL NORT
ORBIS
INDIA

# Zhang Qian

*by Ehren and Riley*

Did you know that a famous Chinese explorer went to jail twice? The first time he went to jail, it took him 10 years to escape. His name was Zhang Qian and even though he went to jail, he still carried out his mission. Qian explored China and other parts of Asia.

Zhang Qian was born in Chennga, China, during the second century BCE. Qian was sent out from Chang'an, the capital of the Han Dynasty in 138 BCE. He had been ordered to find the Yuezhi people. He needed to unite with them against the Xiongnu people. But on Qian's way the Xiongnu people captured him. They put him in jail. He stayed in jail from 138 to 128 BCE. In jail he was given a wife who escaped with him. But Qian was captured again in 126 BCE. He managed to escape a year later and continued on his mission west to find the Yuezhi people.

Qian returned to Chang'an in 125 BCE. He had been away for 13 years. In 119 BCE Qian set out on his second journey to the western parts of China. He was the first person to explore along what is now known as the Silk Road, which is a trading route between China and the Mediterranean countries. Qian died in 114 BCE. His explorations led to the sharing of ideas between eastern China and the world.

# Leif Eriksson

*by Aayush and Makenely*

Do you know who the first European was to find North America? It was Leif Eriksson. Born around 980 in Iceland, Eriksson's father was Erik the Red. Erik the Red captured a German man, Thyrker, and took him back to Iceland. But Erik the Red did not make him a slave. Instead, he sent his son Leif to stay with Thyrker, who would be his teacher. Leif was taught reading, writing in runes, and how to use weapons. Runes are letters in the ancient Norse alphabet.

When Leif Eriksson grew up, he became an explorer. He had heard stories about faraway lands. He wanted to set sail and find them. The first land Eriksson discovered was covered with flat rock slabs. He called the land Helluland. Today it is known as Baffin Island in Canada. The next land he discovered was flat and wooded. It also had white sandy beaches. The land was called Markland. Markland was in Labrador, which is now part of northern Canada.

After he left Markland, Eriksson and his crew found a new land. They built houses on the new land. There were many resources such as salmon. The land was called Vinland. Vinland is on the tip of Newfoundland, which is part of North America.

The great Norse explorer Leif Eriksson died in 1025. He had many adventures. What would the world be like if Eriksson hadn't set sail on his adventures to discover new lands?

## Important Dates about Leif Eriksson

- 980 — *born*

  *has two brothers and one sister*
- 1000 — *sets out on his journey west of Greenland*
- 1950–1960 — *researchers find ruins of his settlement on the tip of Newfoundland*
- 1964 — *U.S. president declares October 9 Leif Eriksson Day*

# Juan Ponce de León

*by David, Jason, and Mason*

Juan Ponce de León was the first European to set foot in Florida. When Ponce de León arrived in Florida in the 1500s, he claimed the land for Spain and named it La Florida. Before that time he went on to accomplish many things.

Ponce de León was born in 1460 in Spain. As a boy he was taught to be a knight. In 1493 Ponce de León went along with Christopher Columbus on a journey to America. Then in 1509, Ponce de León helped defeat the Taino tribe living on the island of Hispaniola. As a reward, Ponce de León was made governor of Puerto Rico. He was also named governor because of his discovery of gold in Puerto Rico.

In 1513 Ponce de León set sail to explore what is now Florida. In 1521 he went back to Florida to start a settlement. He fought with American Indians living there, was wounded, and later died.

Juan Ponce de León bravely explored lands Europeans had never seen before. He led the way for the Spanish to settle in Florida.

## What Is the Fountain of Youth?

The story of Ponce de León looking for the fountain of youth is a myth. He was looking for the Taino tribe, treasure, and land. People made up the story of the Fountain of Youth years after Ponce de León's death.

# The Adventures of Samuel de Champlain

*by Bridget, Ellie, Riley*

French explorer Samuel de Champlain is famous for founding New France in North America. Today New France is part of what is known as Canada. In addition to that, he founded the city of Quebec, Canada.

In 1603 Champlain sailed from France to North America for the first time. Later, in 1608, Champlain built three buildings and surrounded the buildings with a 15-foot wide moat. What Champlain made would become the city of Quebec.

Champlain made many trips across the Atlantic Ocean between New France and France. Each time Champlain would explore more of North America, making maps of the Atlantic Coast, the St. Lawrence River, and the Great Lakes.

By October 1635 Champlain was very sick. He died two months later on Christmas. Champlain was buried at the Notre Dame church in Quebec. Champlain is remembered as a brave explorer of the New World.

# Lewis and Clark

*by Amilia and Audrey*

Meriwether Lewis and William Clark explored much of the western part of today's United States. Lewis and Clark had to explore the west because of the Louisiana Purchase. The Louisiana Purchase was a deal between U.S. President Thomas Jefferson and France in 1803. The agreement gave the United States much of the land in western North America. Lewis and Clark were sent out by President Jefferson in order to find out what was in this new territory.

**A map shows the area of land known as the Louisiana Purchase.**

Lewis and Clark's expedition was called the Corps of Discovery. On the expedition, they met Sacagawea, a daughter of a Shoshone chief, and her husband, French-Canadian Toussiant Charbonneau. They helped Lewis and Clark's group travel westward. The group traveled from Missouri all the way to the Pacific Ocean, arriving in November 1805. They returned home on September 23, 1806.

During their journey they achieved many things. For example, they discovered 178 new plants and 122 species and subspecies of new animals. They helped map the land and brought back information about the people already living in the new territory.

Lewis and Clark led an important expedition and accomplished it in a little over two years. Without Lewis and Clark, we might not have discovered the West.

Meriwether Lewis
Sacagawea
William Clark

# Amelia Earhart

*by Addyson and Susan*

Amelia Earhart was the first woman to fly alone across the Atlantic and Pacific Oceans. Earhart was brave flying through the skies. Earhart's inspiration started by watching airplane stunt shows when she was young. Then one day she took a 10-minute plane ride and knew what she wanted to do: She wanted to fly! Amelia made many flights after that. Soon enough, she had saved enough money to buy her own airplane. In 1932 Earhart flew alone across the Atlantic Ocean. Then in 1935 she flew alone across the Pacific Ocean.

Earhart had an even bigger goal. She wanted to fly around the world. She set out with her navigator, Fred Noonan. He would help read the maps during their trip. On July 2, 1937, Earhart and Noonan got lost between New Guinea and Howland Island, which is between Australia and Hawaii. Their plane went missing. Even though the Navy searched and searched, they never found the plane or Earhart and Noonan's bodies.

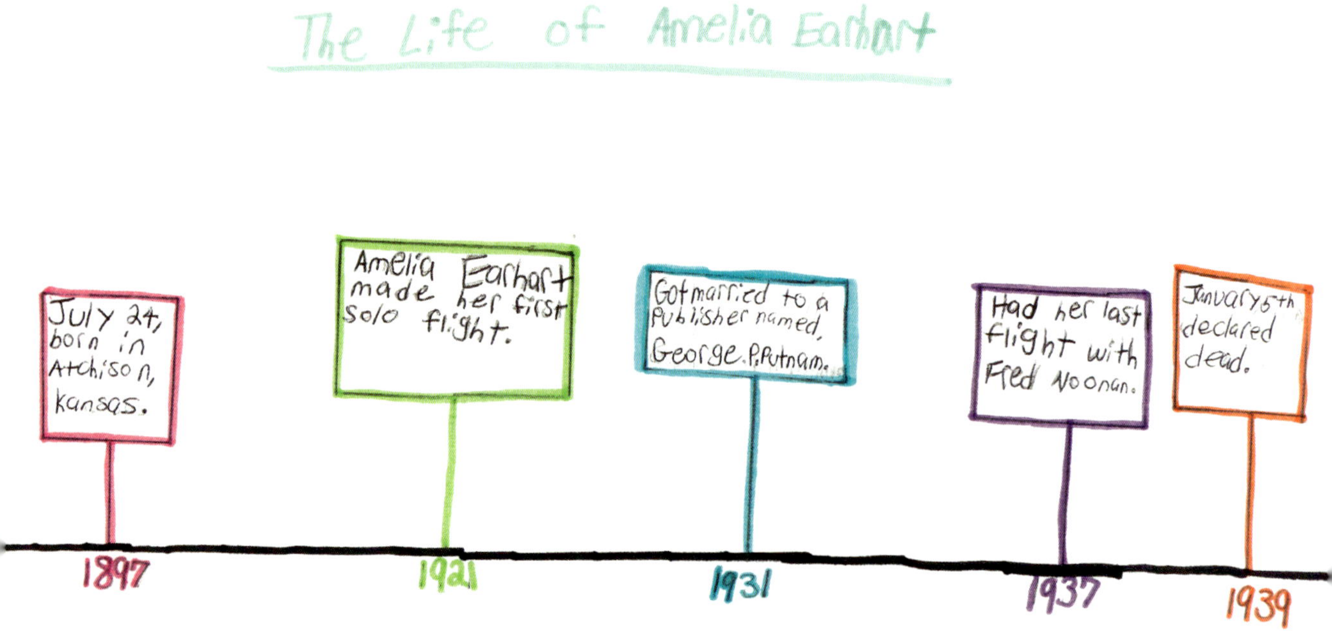

Earhart did not accomplish her final goal, but she is remembered for her courage. People call Earhart "The First Lady of the Air."

**Fascinating Facts!**

Some people think that Amelia and Fred were taken by the Japanese and others think that the President sent them on a private mission.

Did you know that there is a place in Miami, Florida called Amelia Earhart Park?

# Neil Armstrong

*by James and James*

Neil Armstrong was the first person to walk on the moon. This famous space explorer and astronaut was born August 5, 1930. His love of adventure started as a child with an interest in airplanes and flying. At age 15 Armstrong got his pilot's license. A few years later, Armstrong would fight in the Korean War with the U.S. Navy. When he came home, he went to college to study aerospace engineering.

In September 1962, Armstrong joined the astronaut corps at NASA. On December 23, 1968, Armstrong was offered to command Apollo 11. This mission would put humans on the moon. After months and months of training, Apollo 11 launched at Kennedy Space Center in Florida on July 16, 1969. When Armstrong and Buzz Aldrin finally got to the moon, they went exploring. Armstrong was the first to step on the moon's surface.

After Apollo 11, Armstrong held many positions at NASA. Additionally, he was a professor of aerospace engineering at the University of Cincinnati. Armstrong died August 25, 2012. He had a dream and a journey and ended up being the first person to step on the moon.

**Armstrong and Aldrin placed a U.S. flag on the surface of the moon.**

# Sylvia Earle

*by Elise and Garret*

Underwater explorer Sylvia Earle swam her way into the ocean frontier. In 1970 Earle led a team of ocean explorers to the bottom of the ocean to an underwater science lab. Earle went to the bottom of the ocean in a special kind of suit called a Jim. A Jim suit can weigh 1,000 pounds. She went to the bottom in a submarine called *Star II* in 1974. Then in 1979, she did the world's deepest one-person dive of 1,250 feet.

Earle also has accomplishments on land. First, she helped start Deep Ocean Engineering in 1981. Next, she was the head scientist for the National Oceanic and Atmospheric Administration from 1990 to 1991. She has gone on to write books about her underwater explorations. She wrote *Sea Change* and *Exploring the Deep Frontier: The Adventure of Men in the Sea*. She also published *Dive!*; *Hello, Fish!*; and *Sea Critters*.

Sylvia Earle has helped the world learn more about our underwater frontier. Earle knows there are still many ocean discoveries to be made.

# Conclusion

*by Eden and Delilah*

The United States, space, and the deep ocean are all frontiers that were discovered by explorers. These explorers went days without eating or sleeping just to reach their goal. They conquered anyone or anything that got in their way. But look at where they ended up: They're in today's history books! Which explorers do you find most fascinating? Why?